SWAMI VIVEKANANDA

LEGENDS AND LEGACIES

THE BIOGRAPHY OF
SWAMI VIVEKANANDA

Published by
Rupa Publications India Pvt. Ltd 2024
161-B/4, Gulmohar House,
Yusuf Sarai Community Centre,
New Delhi 110049

Sales centres:
Bengaluru Chennai
Hyderabad Kolkata Mumbai

Copyright © Rupa Publications India Pvt. Ltd 2024

The views and opinions expressed in this book are the authors' own and the facts are as reported by him which have been verified to the extent possible, and the publishers are not in any way liable for the same.
All rights reserved.

No part of this publication may be reproduced, transmitted, or stored in a retrieval system, in any form or by any means, electronic, mechanical, photocopying, recording or otherwise, without the prior permission of the publisher.

P-ISBN: 978-93-6156-115-3
E-ISBN: 978-93-6156-628-8

Second impression 2026

10 9 8 7 6 5 4 3 2

Printed in India

This book is sold subject to the condition that it shall not, by way of trade or otherwise, be lent, resold, hired out, or otherwise circulated, without the publisher's prior consent, in any form of binding or cover other than that in which it is published.

Contents

Introduction	7
Swami Vivekananda: Life, Works, and Legacy	9
The Chicago Addresses	25
Principles of Karma Yoga	33
Ideals of Karma Yoga	38
Foundations of Hinduism	43
Religious Philosophy	46
Indian Religious Thought	52
Insights from the Gita	54
Preparations for Higher Life	59
The Life of a Sannyasin	65
Philosophical Teachings	68
From Colombo to Almora	74

Introduction

Hey there, young explorers! Have you ever heard of a real-life superhero named Swami Vivekananda? He wasn't like the ones you see in movies, but he had a superpower of his own—he inspired millions! Swami Vivekananda, also known as the "Cyclonic Monk," was someone who made a huge impact on our world.

Imagine living in a bustling city with a blend of traditional values and new Western influences. That's how Swami Vivekananda started his life in Kolkata, India. His dad was a progressive lawyer, and his mom was a loving homemaker. Even though his family was comfortable, Vivekananda was rich in dreams. He was curious, hardworking, and super into philosophy. And guess what? He didn't let anything stop him.

Here's a beautiful quote from Swami Vivekananda that shows his attitude: **"Arise, awake, and stop not till the goal is reached."** Sounds intense, but it just means that to achieve great things, you have to be determined and persistent.

Vivekananda attended local schools and eventually studied Western philosophy and science. He dreamed of understanding life's big questions, and he found his answers in spirituality. Instead of staying in his comfort zone, he joined Sri Ramakrishna, a mystic who taught him about the unity of all religions and the power of love and service. Pretty cool, right?

One of his biggest achievements was speaking at the Parliament of the World's Religions in Chicago in 1893. Imagine standing in front of people from all over the world and sharing the wisdom of your culture—that's the kind of stuff Vivekananda did! His speech made everyone listen and think about religious tolerance and universal acceptance.

Here's a motivational thought from Vivekananda that might make you smile: **"You have to grow from the inside out. None can teach you, none can make you spiritual. There is no other teacher but your own soul."** Sounds deep, but it just means that true growth comes from within.

Swami Vivekananda wasn't just a monk; he was also a social reformer. He believed in education, equality, and helping the poor. He spent time with people from all walks of life, encouraging them to dream big. He often said, **"Take up one idea. Make that one idea your life—think of it, dream of it, live on that idea. Let the brain, muscles, nerves, every part of your body be full of that idea, and just leave every other idea alone. This is the way to success."**

Even after his travels, Swami Vivekananda continued to inspire others. He founded the Ramakrishna Mission, which is dedicated to social service and spiritual growth. One of his famous quotes is, **"The world is the great gymnasium where we come to make ourselves strong."** He wanted everyone to follow their dreams and never give up.

Life lessons from Swami Vivekananda: it doesn't matter where you start as long as you know where you want to go and work hard to get there. So, keep dreaming big, stay curious, and remember that with dedication and hard work, you can achieve amazing things too!

1

Swami Vivekananda: Life, Works, and Legacy

Birth and Family

Swami Vivekananda, originally named Narendranath Datta, was born on January 12, 1863, into a well-to-do and influential family in Kolkata (then Calcutta). His birth took place at 3 Gourmohan Mukherjee Street, a house that was filled with joy and auspicious rituals on the arrival of a child destined to become a spiritual luminary. Narendranath, affectionately called "Naren," was born into a time of significant cultural and political changes in India, a period that saw the blending of traditional Indian values with new Western influences.

This photograph of Swami Vivekananda was taken in 1896 at Ellys Studio, London

Vishwanath Datta: A Father of Progressive Ideals

Narendranath's father, Vishwanath Datta, was a prominent attorney at the Calcutta High Court, renowned for his legal acumen and progressive thinking. Vishwanath was not just a successful lawyer but also a man of intellect and broad perspectives. He was well-versed in both Eastern and Western philosophy, a rare combination that shaped his worldview and subsequently influenced his household. Vishwanath's library was filled with books on various subjects, including literature, philosophy, and science, reflecting his eclectic interests and intellectual curiosity. He encouraged open discussions and debates at home, fostering an environment where ideas and knowledge were freely exchanged.

> **Fun Fact:**
> **A Renaissance Man:**
> Swami Vivekananda's vast knowledge and intellectual versatility enriched his spiritual teachings and broadened their appeal.

Vishwanath's liberal views extended beyond his professional life. He was an advocate for social reform and supported movements aimed at improving the condition of women and the underprivileged. His progressive stance on social issues and his belief in rational thinking and human dignity deeply impacted young Narendranath. Vishwanath's emphasis on critical thinking and rationality laid the groundwork for Narendranath's intellectual development, encouraging him to question established norms and seek deeper truths.

Bhuvaneshwari Devi: A Mother of Spiritual Depth

Narendranath's mother, Bhuvaneshwari Devi, was a pious and devout woman with a strong inclination towards spirituality. She hailed from a devout Brahmin family, and her life was steeped in religious practices and devotion. Bhuvaneshwari Devi's influence on Narendranath was profound and lasting. She instilled in him the values of compassion, faith, and devotion from a very young age, teaching him the importance of prayer, meditation, and moral integrity.

Bhuvaneshwari Devi's spiritual practices included regular worship, reading of scriptures, and observance of religious festivals with great fervor. She often told Narendranath stories from the epics, Puranas, and the lives of saints, nurturing his imagination and planting the seeds of spiritual curiosity. Her unwavering faith in God and her calm demeanor in the face of life's challenges provided a model of spiritual strength and resilience for Narendranath.

A Balanced Environment for Growth

The combination of his father's rational outlook and his mother's religious devotion created a balanced environment that nurtured Narendranath's intellectual and spiritual growth. This unique upbringing allowed him to develop a holistic perspective, blending the rational and the spiritual in a harmonious way. The Datta household was a confluence of cultures and ideas, reflecting the broader societal changes occurring in India during the 19th century.

> **Fun Fact:**
>
> **Bringing Yoga to the West:** Swami Vivekananda introduced Yoga to the Western world, emphasizing its holistic benefits for physical, mental, and spiritual well-being.

Vishwanath and Bhuvaneshwari Devi's complementary influences equipped Narendranath with a broad and inclusive worldview. From his father, he inherited a love for knowledge, critical inquiry, and a progressive outlook on social issues. From his mother, he received the gifts of faith, devotion, and an innate understanding of spirituality. This dual heritage prepared him for his future role as a spiritual leader and social reformer.

Early Signs of Greatness

From an early age, Narendranath exhibited signs of exceptional intelligence and curiosity. He was known for his prodigious memory, keen observation skills, and an insatiable thirst for knowledge. Family members and visitors often marveled at his ability to grasp complex concepts and his articulate expression of ideas. His playful nature, combined with a deep sense of empathy and kindness, endeared him to everyone around him.

> **Fun Fact:**
> **Mentoring Western Disciples:** Swami Vivekananda mentored several Western disciples, including Sister Nivedita, who significantly contributed to Indian education and women's empowerment.

Despite his playful and sometimes mischievous nature, young Narendranath displayed an unusual depth of thought and reflection. He would often spend hours in contemplation, pondering the mysteries of life and existence. These early signs of intellectual brilliance and spiritual inclination hinted at the remarkable path that lay ahead of him.

Cultural and Social Influences

The cultural and social milieu of Kolkata during Narendranath's childhood played a significant role in shaping his character and worldview. Kolkata, the capital of British India at the time, was a melting pot of cultures, ideas, and political movements. The city was a hub of intellectual activity, witnessing the convergence of traditional Indian thought and modern Western ideas. This dynamic environment exposed Narendranath to a wide range of influences, from the literary and philosophical to the socio-political.

The Datta family's active engagement with contemporary social and intellectual currents provided Narendranath with a rich tapestry of experiences. He was exposed to the works of prominent thinkers, reformers, and literary figures of the time. This exposure broadened his horizons and deepened his understanding of the world, preparing him for the pivotal role he would play in the spiritual and cultural renaissance of India.

Education and Intellectual Development

Narendranath's formal education began at the Metropolitan Institution, where he demonstrated exceptional academic abilities. His inquisitive mind and sharp intellect were evident from a young age. He later attended the Scottish Church College, where he excelled in various subjects, including Western philosophy, history, and science. His fascination with Western thought was matched by his deep interest in Indian scriptures and philosophy. This dual interest led him to explore and question the nature of existence, reality, and spirituality.

Stamp image from Swami Vivekananda (1863-1902) on his 150th Birth Anniversary and Dakshineswar Kali Temple, released 2013 in India.

Credits: Post of India

He was particularly drawn to the works of John Stuart Mill, David Hume, and Herbert Spencer, whose writings inspired him to think critically and question established norms. However, despite his academic success, Narendranath felt an inner void and yearned for deeper spiritual understanding.

Spiritual Quest

Narendranath's quest for spiritual knowledge was intense and unrelenting. He explored various religious paths and sought answers from different spiritual leaders. His search for truth led him to the Brahmo Samaj, an influential socio-religious reform movement of the time, where he met Keshab Chandra Sen, a prominent leader of the movement. Although he was initially impressed by the rational and reformist approach of the Brahmo Samaj, Narendranath soon realized that it did not fulfill his spiritual aspirations. His inner turmoil and longing for spiritual enlightenment continued to grow.

TRANSFORMATION INTO SWAMI VIVEKANANDA

Meeting Sri Ramakrishna

The turning point in Narendranath's life came in 1881 when he met Sri Ramakrishna Paramahamsa, a mystic and saint residing at the Dakshineswar Kali Temple. Sri Ramakrishna's simple yet profound teachings deeply resonated with Narendranath. Unlike the philosophical debates and intellectual discussions he was accustomed to, Sri Ramakrishna's spiritual insights were based on direct personal experience. Initially skeptical, Narendranath tested Sri Ramakrishna's authenticity by asking him if he had seen God. Sri Ramakrishna's unequivocal affirmation and his vivid description of his mystical experiences convinced Narendranath of the truth in his words. This meeting marked the beginning of a profound transformation in Narendranath's life. Under Sri Ramakrishna's guidance, he underwent rigorous spiritual training, which included intense meditation, devotion, and service. Sri Ramakrishna taught him the unity of all religions and the realization of God through love and devotion.

Spiritual Training and Renunciation

Narendranath's transformation into Swami Vivekananda was marked by a period of intense spiritual discipline and self-realization. He immersed himself in the teachings of Sri Ramakrishna, embracing a monastic life and renouncing worldly attachments. His days were filled with meditation, study of scriptures, and service to his guru. He often engaged in deep discussions with Sri Ramakrishna, who guided him through various spiritual experiences and realizations. The rigorous training helped Narendranath attain a state of spiritual awakening, where he experienced the divine presence in all aspects of life. This transformation was not just an internal journey but also a preparation for his future mission to spread the teachings of Vedanta and the message of universal brotherhood.

Establishing the Ramakrishna Order

After the passing of Sri Ramakrishna in 1886, Swami Vivekananda, along with his fellow disciples, established the Ramakrishna Math at Baranagar in North Kolkata. This monastic order was dedicated to spiritual practice and the service of humanity, embodying the teachings of their revered guru. The early days of the Math were marked by extreme austerity and simplicity. The monks lived a life of poverty, devoting themselves to meditation, study, and service. Swami Vivekananda's leadership and vision were instrumental in shaping the order's direction and objectives. He emphasized the importance of selfless service, education, and spiritual practice, laying the foundation for a movement that would grow to have a global impact.

JOURNEY TO THE WEST

The Call to America

Swami Vivekananda's journey to the West began with an inner calling to spread the message of Vedanta and Hindu philosophy to a broader audience. In 1893, he traveled to the United States to attend the Parliament of the World's Religions in Chicago. Despite facing numerous challenges, including financial difficulties and cultural barriers, he persevered, driven by his mission to promote universal brotherhood and religious harmony. His arrival in America marked the beginning of a new in his life, where he would gain international recognition and acclaim for his teachings.

Parliament of the World's Religions

Swami Vivekananda's historic address at the Parliament of the World's Religions on September 11, 1893, was a defining moment. His eloquent speech, beginning with the words "Sisters and Brothers of America," received a standing ovation and established him as a prominent spiritual leader. He spoke about the essence of Hinduism, the principles of Vedanta, and the importance of religious tolerance and universal acceptance. His message resonated deeply with the audience, highlighting the unity of all religions and the need for mutual respect and understanding. This event marked the beginning of Swami Vivekananda's extensive lecture tours across the United States and Europe, where he continued to inspire and educate people from all walks of life.

Lectures and Teachings in the West

Swami Vivekananda's lectures and teachings in the West covered a wide range of topics, including spirituality, philosophy, and social issues. He established Vedanta Societies in several cities, fostering a deeper understanding of Eastern spirituality among Western audiences. His teachings emphasized the practical application of Vedanta principles in daily life, encouraging individuals to realize their inherent divinity and work towards self-improvement and service to humanity. His charisma, eloquence, and profound insights attracted a large following, including prominent intellectuals, artists, and social reformers. Swami Vivekananda's impact on Western thought was significant, as he introduced a holistic view of spirituality that transcended religious and cultural boundaries.

> **Fun Fact:**
> **Extensive Travels and Global Influence:** Swami Vivekananda travelled extensively, bridging the gap between East and West through lectures and interactions, promoting Indian spirituality globally.

Publications and Writings

In addition to his lectures, Swami Vivekananda made substantial contributions to literature. His writings, including books, essays, and letters, provide comprehensive insights into the various paths of spiritual practice. His major works, such as "Raja Yoga," "Karma Yoga," "Jnana Yoga," and "Bhakti Yoga," offer detailed explanations of the different aspects of yoga and their relevance to personal and spiritual growth. These works continue to inspire and educate people worldwide, making complex spiritual concepts accessible to a broad audience. Swami Vivekananda's literary legacy serves as a valuable resource for anyone seeking to understand and apply the principles of Vedanta in their lives.

RETURN TO INDIA AND NATIONALISTIC ACTIVITIES

Homecoming and Reception

Swami Vivekananda returned to India in 1897, where he received a hero's welcome. His successful mission in the West had brought immense pride to his countrymen, who saw him as a symbol of India's spiritual heritage and intellectual prowess. Upon his return, Swami Vivekananda embarked on a mission to revive the spirit of his nation and address the social and economic challenges facing his people. He emphasized the need for education, social reform, and the upliftment of the marginalized sections of society.

> **Fun Fact:**
> **Authoring Philosophical Works:** Swami Vivekananda's works, like "Raja Yoga," "Karma Yoga," and "Jnana Yoga," remain influential texts in spiritual literature.

Founding the Ramakrishna Mission

In May 1897, Swami Vivekananda founded the Ramakrishna Mission, a philanthropic and spiritual organization dedicated to the service of humanity. The Mission's activities included establishing schools, colleges, hospitals, and rural development programs. Swami Vivekananda believed that education was the

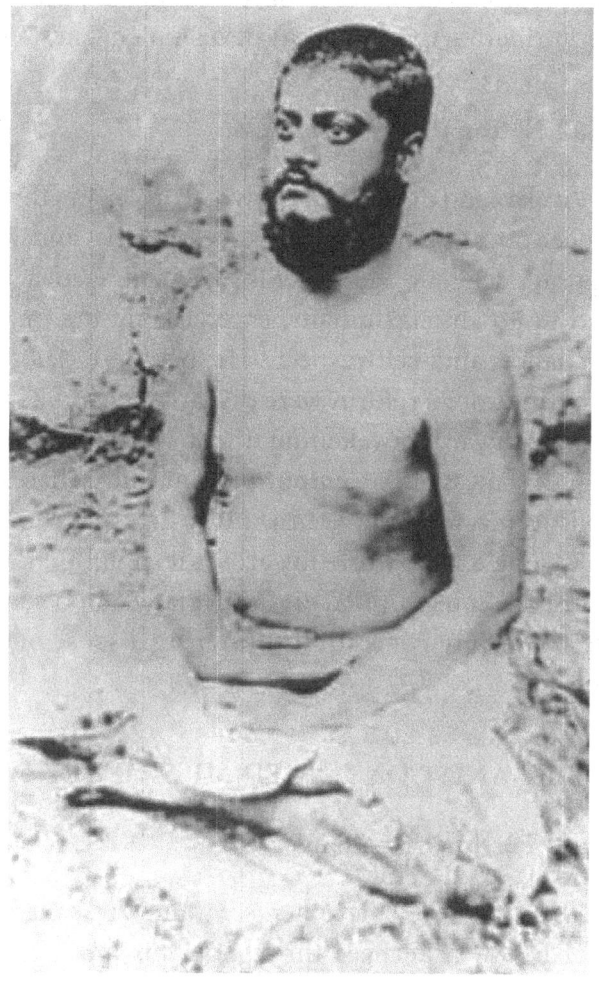

Image of Swami Vivekananda in Cossipore

key to India's progress and worked tirelessly to promote it. The Ramakrishna Mission aimed to provide holistic education that included physical, mental, and spiritual development. It also focused on healthcare, disaster relief, and social welfare, embodying the principles of selfless service and compassion. The Mission's work continues to have a lasting impact on Indian society, contributing to the nation's development and well-being.

Promoting National Consciousness

Swami Vivekananda played a pivotal role in the Indian renaissance, promoting national consciousness and inspiring contemporary leaders. His teachings encouraged a sense of pride and unity among Indians, emphasizing the importance of self-reliance and self-respect. He believed that spiritual awakening and social reform were essential for India's progress and worked towards awakening the national spirit. Swami Vivekananda's message of empowerment and self-realization resonated deeply with the youth, inspiring many to join the freedom struggle and work towards the upliftment of their nation. His vision of a united and spiritually empowered India continues to inspire generations, fostering a sense of national pride and identity.

LATER LIFE AND CONTINUED MISSIONARY WORK

Health and Personal Challenges

Despite his numerous achievements, Swami Vivekananda faced significant health challenges throughout his life. His rigorous schedule, extensive travel, and the demands of his mission took a toll on his health. He suffered from asthma, diabetes, and other ailments, yet he continued his work with unwavering determination. Swami Vivekananda's resilience and dedication to his mission were evident in his relentless efforts to spread the message of Vedanta and serve humanity, even in the face of personal hardships.

Influence on Indian Society and Independence Movement

Swami Vivekananda's ideas and teachings significantly influenced Indian society and the independence movement. His call for national awakening and self-reliance resonated with leaders and freedom fighters, including Mahatma Gandhi, Subhas Chandra Bose, and Jawaharlal Nehru. Swami Vivekananda's vision of a spiritually and morally empowered India inspired many to work towards social reform and the upliftment of the marginalized. His emphasis on education, social service, and the revival of Indian culture contributed to shaping modern Indian identity. Swami Vivekananda's legacy continues to inspire efforts towards social justice, national pride, and the pursuit of spiritual growth.

> **Fun Fact:**
> **Promoting the Unity of Science and Religion:** Swami Vivekananda believed in the complementary nature of science and religion, inspiring exploration of their intersection.

Key Disciples and Followers

The disciples and followers of Swami Vivekananda, who come from various backgrounds, represent a diverse and energetic group of persons who embody the universal appeal of his teachings. Both Western converts, such as Captain Thomas A. Anderson, and devout Indian devotees, like Sarat Chandra Chakravarty, played crucial roles in disseminating Vedanta. Their endeavours, ranging from establishing ashrams to providing assistance to Vedanta centres, demonstrate their steadfast dedication to Vivekananda's concept of spiritual harmony and philanthropic work.

Charlotte Sevier (1847–20 October 1930) was a devoted disciple of Swami Vivekananda. With her husband, Captain James Henry Sevier, she established the Advaita Ashrama in Mayavati. The couple met Vivekananda during his second visit to London and became ardent followers. They joined him on a European tour in 1896, which inspired them to establish the Ashrama. After her husband's death in 1900, Charlotte continued managing the Ashrama, editing the Prabuddha Bharata magazine, and supporting the Vivekananda Ashrama and Memorial Temple Fund.

Alasinga Perumal (1865–11 May 1909) was a fervent propagator of Vedanta and a dedicated follower of Swami Vivekananda. Born in Chikkamagalur, he played a crucial role in Vivekananda's participation in the 1893 Parliament of the World's Religions, raising funds for the Swami's journey to America. He also founded the Brahmavadin journal to spread Vedanta teachings.

Sister Nivedita (Margaret Elizabeth Noble; 28 October 1867–13 October 1911) was an Irish teacher and social activist. She met Vivekananda in London in 1895 and was profoundly impacted by his teachings. In India, she opened a girls' school in Calcutta, nursed patients during the 1899 plague, and supported Indian nationalism and science, notably aiding Jagadish Chandra Bose.

Swami Nischayananda (11 May 1865–22 October 1934), born Suraj Rao, was an Indian monk and disciple of Vivekananda. After financial struggles and a military career, he embraced monasticism. He served the sick and poor alongside Swami

Kalyanananda at the Ramakrishna Mission Sevashrama in Kankhal.

Alberta Montagu, Countess of Sandwich (7 September 1877 – 23 October 1951), an American heiress, was a close friend and devotee of Vivekananda. Known for hosting Vivekananda at her family's estate, she supported his work in the West. Despite her aristocratic responsibilities, she remained a dedicated supporter throughout her life.

Josephine MacLeod (1858–15 October 1949), known as "Tantine" and "Jo Jo," was an American friend and devotee of Vivekananda. Her support was invaluable, providing financial aid to the Ramakrishna Order and promoting Vedanta in the West. She also supported Sister Nivedita's work and continued to champion Vivekananda's teachings after his death.

Raja Ajit Singh of Khetri (16 October 1861–18 January 1901) was the ruler of Khetri and a close friend and disciple of Vivekananda. His financial assistance was instrumental in Vivekananda's participation in the Parliament of the World's Religions, helping spread Vedanta globally.

Swami Abhayananda , also known as Captain Thomas A. Anderson, was an American disciple of Swami Vivekananda. Inspired by Vivekananda's teachings on Vedanta and spiritual discipline, he became one of the first Westerners to embrace Hindu monasticism. Swami Abhayananda dedicated his life to spreading Vedanta in the West, translating key texts, and giving lectures to introduce Western audiences to Hindu philosophy and meditation practices.

Betty Leggett , born Elizabeth Sturges, was the daughter of Alberta Montagu's stepfather, Francis H. Leggett. She was deeply influenced by Swami Vivekananda's teachings and was a devoted follower. Betty supported the Vedanta movement through her connections and resources, aiding in the establishment of Vedanta centers and contributing to the dissemination of Vivekananda's message in the West.

Sara Chapman Bull (1850-1911), also known as Dhira Mata, was an American musician and philanthropist who became a devoted follower of Swami Vivekananda. After meeting him in 1894, she became an ardent supporter of his mission, providing financial and organizational assistance. She played a significant role in introducing Vedanta to the Western world, hosting Vivekananda's lectures and promoting his ideas through various social and intellectual circles.

Sarat Chandra Chakravarty (1869-1935) was an Indian disciple of Swami Vivekananda. A teacher and writer, he documented many of Vivekananda's teachings and interactions with disciples, providing valuable insights into the Swami's philosophy and work. Sarat Chandra's writings and lectures helped preserve and propagate Vivekananda's teachings, making them accessible to a wider audience in India.

Swami Nischayananda (11 May 1865-22 October 1934), born Suraj Rao, was an Indian monk and a direct disciple of Swami Vivekananda. After facing financial difficulties and serving in the military, he was inspired by Vivekananda and Swami Niranjanananda to embrace monastic life. Nischayananda dedicated himself to serving the poor and sick, working at the Ramakrishna Mission Sevashrama in Kankhal. His commitment to humanitarian work exemplified the ideals of the Ramakrishna Order.

2

The Chicago Addresses

Response to Welcome, Why We Disagree, Paper on Hinduism (19 Sept 1893), Religion Not the Crying Need of India (20 Sept 1893), Buddhism the Fulfilment of Hinduism (26 Sept 1893), Address at the Final Session (27 Sept 1893)

At the World's Parliament of Religions in Chicago on 11 September 1893, Swami Vivekananda delivered an address filled with gratitude and profound wisdom, starting with the heartfelt salutation, **"Sisters and Brothers of America."** The room was electric with the significance of the moment, a meeting of minds and souls from diverse religious backgrounds. Vivekananda, embodying the essence of India's ancient spiritual traditions, rose to the occasion with a sense of profound reverence and joy. He expressed his overwhelming joy and thanked the audience on behalf of the ancient order of monks and millions of Hindus. **"It fills my heart with joy unspeakable to rise in response to the warm and cordial welcome which you have given us,"** he began, his voice resonating with sincerity and gratitude. He extended his thanks not only on behalf of the ancient order of monks but also in the name of the mother of religions and millions of Hindu people from all classes and sects.

Emphasising the essence of Hinduism, he proudly declared, **"I am proud to belong to a religion which has taught the world both tolerance and universal acceptance."** This statement was more than a proclamation; it was a testament to the inclusivity and expansive nature of Hinduism. Vivekananda highlighted India's historical embrace of persecuted people, including Jews and Zoroastrians, who found refuge in the country during times of great distress. **"I am proud to belong to a nation which has sheltered the persecuted and the refugees of all religions and all nations of the earth,"** he declared with pride. He recounted how the Israelites came to southern India and took refuge during the Roman tyranny that destroyed their holy temple. Similarly, he spoke of the Zoroastrians, whose nation was given shelter and continues to thrive in India.

Vivekananda then quoted a hymn that he had recited since childhood, one that is repeated daily by millions: *"As the different streams having their sources in different places all mingle their water in the sea, so, O Lord, the different paths which men take through different tendencies, various though they appear, crooked or straight, all lead to Thee."* This hymn encapsulated the universalism that is central to Hindu philosophy, a belief that all paths, despite their differences, ultimately converge to the same divine source. The present convention, which is one of the most august assemblies ever held, is in itself a vindication, a declaration to the world of the wonderful doctrine preached in the Gita: *"Whosoever comes to Me, through whatsoever form, I reach him; all men are struggling through paths which in the end lead to me."*

> **Fun Fact:**
> **Becoming the Beloved Disciple:** Swami Vivekananda became Ramakrishna's cherished disciple, entrusted with spreading Vedanta and spiritual enlightenment worldwide.

He lamented the destructive power of sectarianism, bigotry, and fanaticism, decrying how these forces have filled the earth with violence, drenched it often and often with human blood, destroyed civilisation, and sent whole nations to despair. His voice grew intense as he spoke of these horrors, expressing his fervent hope that the bell that tolled this morning in honour of this convention may be the death-knell of all fanaticism, of all persecutions with the sword or with the pen, and of all uncharitable feelings between persons wending their way to the same goal. **"Had it not been for these horrible demons, human society would be far more advanced than it is now. But their time has come,"** he declared with conviction.

Sunset captured near Kali Ghat Temple, Kolkata. Vivekananda Setu is a bridge over the Hooghly River, it connects Kolkata city and Dakshineswar.

On 15 September 1893, Vivekananda shared a metaphorical story to illustrate the cause of religious narrow-mindedness and variance. **"I will tell you a little story,"** he began, recounting the tale of a frog in a well who believed his well was the entire world until a sea frog enlightened him about the vastness of the ocean. This story, humorous and insightful, served to illustrate the limitations of perspective and the necessity of broadening one's horizons. "**I am a Hindu. I am sitting in my own little well and thinking that the whole world is my little well,**" Vivekananda confessed, acknowledging the universal tendency to be confined by one's own experiences and beliefs. He praised America's efforts to break down these barriers, expressing hope that in the future, the Lord will help accomplish this noble purpose.

During his Paper on Hinduism on 19 September 1893, Vivekananda delved deeper into the resilience and comprehensive nature of Hinduism. He traced its history, noting that Hinduism, along with Zoroastrianism and Judaism, has withstood tremendous shocks over the centuries, proving their internal strength. "**Three religions now stand in the world, which have come down to us from time prehistoric—Hinduism, Zoroastrianism, and Judaism,**" he stated. While Judaism was unable to absorb Christianity and was driven out of its birthplace, and Zoroastrianism was reduced to a handful of followers, Hinduism faced numerous sects that seemed to shake it to its very foundations. However, like the waters of the seashore in a tremendous earthquake, it receded only for a while, only to return in an all-absorbing flood, a thousand times more vigorous.

Serbian stamp from Swami Vivekananda (1863-1902) 2018.

Credits: Post of Serbia, Public domain, via Wikimedia Commons

Vivekananda highlighted the inclusivity of Hinduism, which accommodates a wide spectrum of beliefs, from the high spiritual flights of the Vedanta philosophy to the low ideas of idolatry. "**From the high** spiritual flights of the Vedanta philosophy, of which the latest discoveries of science seem like echoes, to the low ideas of idolatry with its multifarious mythology, the agnosticism of the Buddhists, and the atheism of the Jains, each and all have a place in the Hindu's religion," he explained. This inclusive nature raises the question of the common centre where all these diverse beliefs converge, a question Vivekananda aimed to answer. He emphasised that Hindus have received their religion through revelation, the Vedas, which are considered without beginning or end. **"The Vedas are without beginning and without end,"** he asserted, comparing them to the law of gravitation, which existed before its discovery and would continue to exist even if forgotten by humanity.

He addressed the concept of creation, asserting that it is without a beginning or end. **"Creation and creator are two lines, without beginning and without end, running parallel to each other,"** he explained. He dismissed the idea of a mutable God, which would imply that God could undergo destruction. Instead, he posited that there never was a time when there was no creation. This cyclical nature of creation and dissolution aligns with modern scientific principles, such as the conservation of cosmic energy. **"The sum total of cosmic energy is always the same,"** he noted.

Vivekananda then turned to the nature of the soul, proclaiming, **"I am a spirit living in a body. I am not the body.**

> **Fun Fact:**
> **The Pivotal Encounter- Meeting Ramakrishna:**
> In 1881, Narendranath met his spiritual mentor, Ramakrishna Paramhansa, at the Dakshineswar Kali Temple. Initially skeptical, he was gradually won over by Ramakrishna's profound spiritual wisdom and unconditional love, leading to a deep bond between them.

The body will die, but I shall not die." He explained that the soul, unlike the body, was not created and therefore cannot die. The disparities in human conditions, he argued, are a result of past actions, adhering to the principle of karma. **"The present is determined by our past actions, and the future by the present,"** he asserted. This view rejects the notion of an arbitrary creator God and instead attributes individual destinies to the cumulative effects of past lives.

He further elaborated on the doctrine of reincarnation, explaining that the soul evolves through a series of births and deaths. **"The soul will go on evolving up or reverting from birth to birth and death to death,"** he stated. This journey is not without hope; the soul can achieve perfection and liberation through purity and divine realization. **"He reveals Himself to the pure heart; the pure and the stainless see God, yea, even in this life,"** he proclaimed, emphasizing the transformative power of spiritual purity.

Vivekananda addressed the philosophical underpinnings of Hinduism, particularly the concept of Advaita, or non-dualism. **"Science has proved to me that physical individuality is a delusion,"** he stated, drawing parallels between scientific unity and spiritual unity. He argued that just as science seeks to find unity in diversity, so does the Hindu philosophy strive to realize the oneness of all existence. **"As soon as science would reach perfect unity, it would stop from further progress, because it would reach the goal,"** he explained, noting that this ultimate unity is the foundation of all existence.

He then transitioned to a critique of religious dogmatism and bigotry. **"Superstition is a great enemy of man, but bigotry is worse,"** he declared. He recounted an anecdote of a Christian missionary preaching in India, who mocked the Hindu practice of idol worship. Vivekananda highlighted the irony and futility of such criticisms, noting that every religion has its symbols and rituals. **"Why does a Christian go to church? Why is the cross holy? Why is the face turned toward the sky in prayer?"** he questioned, emphasizing the universality of symbolic worship.

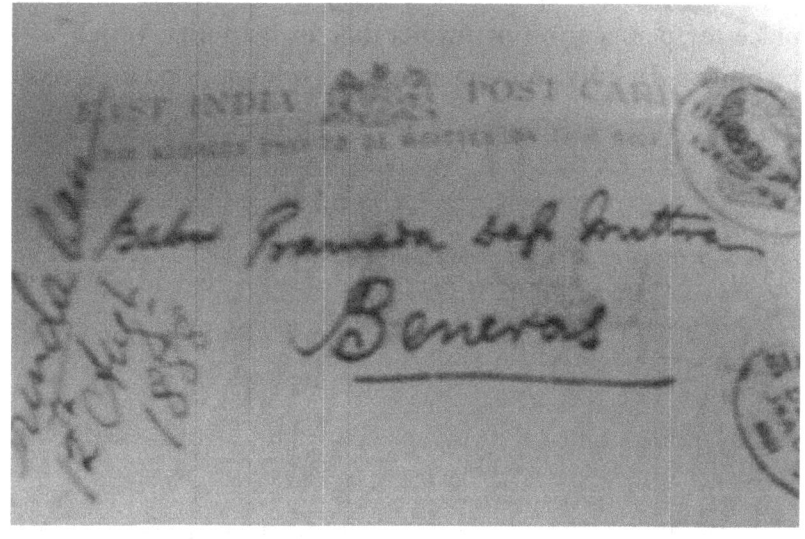

Post card used by Swami Vivekananda (1863-1902) in 1888.

Vivekananda explained that Hinduism views all religions as different paths to the same goal, a progression from lower to higher truths. **"To the Hindu, man is not traveling from error to truth, but from truth to truth, from lower to higher truth,"** he stated. This perspective allows for a harmonious coexistence of diverse beliefs, recognizing that each religion represents an attempt to grasp and realize the Infinite. **"Unity in variety is the plan of nature, and the Hindu has recognized it,"** he declared, advocating for mutual respect and understanding among different faiths.

He concluded his address by envisioning a universal religion that transcends geographical and temporal boundaries. **"If there is ever to be a universal religion, it must be one which will have no location in place or time; which will be infinite like the God it will preach," he proclaimed. This religion would embrace all humanity, recognizing the divine nature within every individual. "It will be a religion which will have no place for persecution or intolerance in its polity, which will recognize divinity in every man and woman," he envisioned.

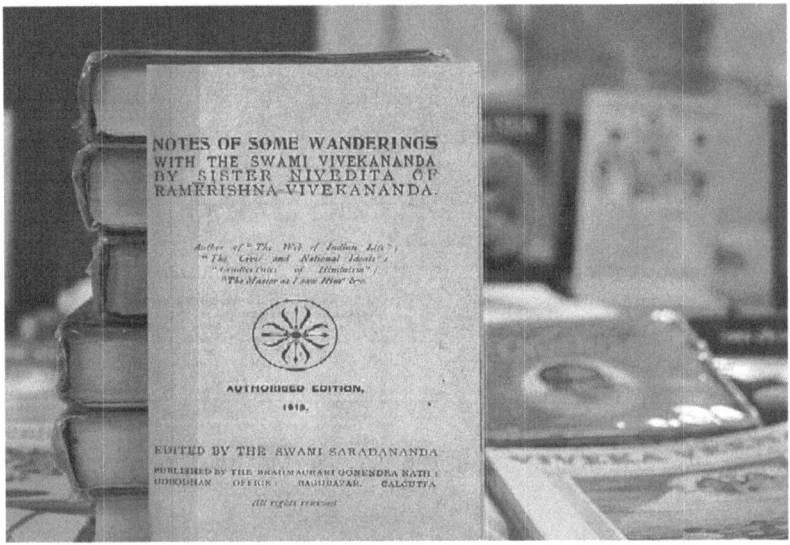

Spiritual significance of sufferings and books of Swami Vivekananda

Credits: Ashish, CC BY 2.0 <https://creativecommons.org/licenses/by/2.0>, via Wikimedia Commons

3

Principles of Karma Yoga

Karma in Its Effect on Character, Each Is Great in His Own Place, The Secret of Work, What Is Duty?, We Help Ourselves, Not the World, Non-Attachment Is the Complete Self-Abnegation

Karma in its effect on character. The word *Karma* is derived from the Sanskrit *Kri*, meaning to do; all action is *Karma*. This word also implies the effects of actions. In metaphysics, it sometimes means the effects of our past actions as causes. But in *Karma-Yoga*, it pertains to work. The goal of mankind is knowledge. That is the ideal placed before us by Eastern philosophy. Pleasure is not the goal but knowledge. Pleasure and happiness are transient. The mistake is thinking that pleasure is the ideal. The cause of all miseries is this foolish pursuit of pleasure. Over time, man finds that it's not happiness but knowledge that he seeks and that both pleasure and pain are great teachers, learning as much from evil as from good. As pleasure and pain pass before the soul, they imprint different pictures, forming a man's **"character"**. Character is the aggregate of

> **Fun Fact:**
> **The Historic Chicago Speech:** On September 11, 1893, Swami Vivekananda's speech at the Parliament of the World's Religions in Chicago introduced Indian spirituality to the West, earning widespread acclaim.

tendencies, the sum total of the mind's bent; happiness and misery are equal factors in character formation. Good and evil equally shape character, with misery sometimes being the greater teacher. In studying great characters, it's often found that misery taught more than happiness, poverty more than wealth, blows more than praise. Knowledge is inherent in man. No knowledge comes from outside; it's all inside. What a man "knows" is what he "discovers" or "unveils" from within his own soul, which is a mine of infinite knowledge. Newton discovered gravitation not by finding it in the apple but by uncovering it within his own mind. All knowledge the world has ever received comes from the mind. The external world merely suggests the occasion to study one's own mind. The falling apple suggested to Newton to study his mind, leading to the discovery of the law of gravitation. Knowledge, secular or spiritual, is in the human mind. Often, it remains covered, and the uncovering process is called learning. The man from whom the veil is lifted is more knowing; the man upon whom it lies thick is ignorant, and the one from whom it has entirely gone is omniscient. Omniscient men have existed and will exist in the future. Like fire in a flint, knowledge exists in the mind; suggestion is the friction that brings it out. So, with all feelings and actions—tears, smiles, joys, griefs, curses, blessings, praises, blames—each arises from within ourselves through life's many blows. This is called *Karma*—work, action. Every blow given to the soul, striking fire from it and discovering its power and knowledge, is *Karma*. We are all doing *Karma* all the time. Talking is *Karma*. Listening

> **Fun Fact:**
> **Founding Vedanta Societies:** Swami Vivekananda founded Vedanta Societies in the U.S. and England, establishing centers for spiritual learning and practice.

is *Karma*. Breathing, walking—all are *Karma* and leave their marks. There are works that aggregate many smaller works. The seashore's waves create noise, each composed of millions of minute waves, each making a noise, but only the big aggregate is heard. Similarly, every heart's pulsation is work, felt and tangible when aggregated. To judge a man's character, watch his most common actions. Every fool may become a hero once; great occasions rouse even the lowest beings to greatness, but the truly great man's character is consistently great. **"Karma in its effect on character is the most tremendous power that man has to deal with."** Man, as a center, attracts all the universe's powers, fusing and sending them off in a big current. This center is the real man—almighty and omniscient—drawing the universe towards him, fashioning character from good, bad, misery, and happiness, throwing it outward. All actions in the world, all human society's movements, all works around us display thought, manifesting man's will. Machines, instruments, cities, ships—all display man's will, caused by character, manufactured by *Karma*. **"As is Karma, so is the manifestation of will."** Great men of mighty will have been tremendous workers, their wills powerful enough to overturn worlds, obtained through persistent work over ages. A Buddha or a Jesus didn't obtain their wills in one life; their fathers were not notable. Millions of carpenters like Joseph and petty kings like Buddha's father existed. If it were hereditary, how did these petty men produce sons worshiped by millions? This accumulation of power must have grown through ages, bursting upon society in a Buddha or a Jesus. All is

> **Fun Fact:**
> **Inspired by the Bhagavad Gita:**
> The Bhagavad Gita significantly influenced Swami Vivekananda's philosophy, integrating its teachings into his message.

determined by *Karma*—work. No one gets anything unless earned. A man may struggle for riches, cheat thousands, but if undeserving, his life becomes a nuisance. Accumulating for physical enjoyment only brings what is earned. A fool may buy all books but read only what he deserves, determined by *Karma*. We are responsible for what we are and can make ourselves whatever we wish by present actions. Learning how to work cleverly and scientifically, obtaining the greatest results, is essential. Work brings out the mind's power, waking the soul. Man works with motives—fame, money, power, heaven, name. Work for work's sake is rare, done because good comes of it. Some help mankind from higher motives, believing and loving good. Unselfishness pays more, but patience is needed to practice it. **"Unselfishness is more paying from the point of view of health also."** Love, truth, and unselfishness are our highest

Drawing Room–Swami Vivekanandas Ancestral House–Kolkata 2011-10-22

Credits: Biswarup Ganguly, CC BY-SA 4.0 <https://creativecommons.org/licenses/by-sa/4.0>, via Wikimedia Commons

ideals, forming the greatest power. A man working without selfish motives can become a moral giant. Self-restraint shows greater power than action. Restraining outgoing energy develops power, producing a mighty will, a Christ or a Buddha. Even a fool may rule the world by working and waiting, restraining foolish ideas. **"Even the lowest forms of work are not to be despised."** All should strive towards higher motives, understanding them. **"To work we have the right, but not to the fruits thereof."** Work without caring for results. Intense activity and calm renunciation balance each other. **"The ideal man finds intense activity in solitude and solitude in intense activity."** Control and self-restraint are keys. Work with unselfishness leads to perfect calmness. Our duty is to encourage every struggle towards the highest ideal. Different stages of life—student, householder, retiree, Sannyasin—each has duties. No stage is superior. **"The scavenger is as great and glorious as the king."** The householder must perform duties, helping others, pure in heart, a hero to enemies, gentle to friends. Acquiring wealth for noble purposes is worship. **"The householder who struggles to become rich by good means for good purposes is attaining salvation."** Encouraging others' struggle towards their ideal, making it as near to truth as possible, is our duty. The ideal of non-resistance teaches that man's duty is to resist evil until non-resistance becomes a virtue. Each is great in their place. Work incessantly, free from selfishness, binding results, and attachment, becoming a powerful moral giant. This is the essence of *Karma-Yoga*."

4

Ideals of Karma Yoga

Freedom, The Ideal of Karma Yoga, Women of India, Soul, God, and Religion

Freedom

Freedom is not merely the absence of restraint but an intricate concept deeply rooted in the philosophy of Karma Yoga. **Karma Yoga**, the path of selfless action, teaches us that freedom can only be achieved through the meticulous balance of cause and effect. The law of Karma, or causation, dictates that every action, thought, and feeling produces an effect, creating a cycle of cause and consequence. This cycle, according to our philosophy, is omnipresent, spanning the entire universe. It implies that everything we experience is both a result of past actions and a cause for future ones. The notion of 'law' in this context is the tendency of a series to repeat itself, which our ancient Nyâya philosophers

Indian stamp from Swami Vivekananda (1863-1902) 2018.

Credits: India Post, Government of India, GODL-India <https://data.gov.in/sites/default/files/Gazette_Notification_OGDL.pdf>, via Wikimedia Commons

refer to as Vyâpti, or pervasiveness of association.

Law, as understood here, is not inherent in nature but a construct of the human mind. It is the mind's method of grasping the recurrence of phenomena, forming a mental association that expects similar outcomes. This psychological aspect of association and causation highlights that law exists only within the conditioned universe characterized by space, time, and causation (Desha-kâla-nimitta). Beyond this conditioned existence, freedom exists unbound by these laws, illustrating the limitation of free will within our universe.

The ideal of freedom encompasses moving beyond these limitations. To attain true freedom, one must relinquish attachment to the transient, conditioned universe. This transcendence, though difficult, can be approached through two paths: the negative way of "Neti Neti" (not this, not this) for those with exceptional willpower, and the positive way of "Iti" (this), which involves experiencing and gradually detaching from the world through knowledge and work. **Karma Yoga** thus becomes a practical approach to attaining freedom by performing actions without attachment, understanding the secret of work, and realizing the ultimate freedom beyond the confines of the material world.

The Ideal of Karma Yoga

Karma Yoga, the ideal of selfless action, teaches the knowledge of work's secret. The entire universe is in a perpetual state of work, striving for liberty, from the atom to the highest being. This relentless pursuit of freedom manifests in various forms, from the physical to the spiritual. Karma Yoga emphasizes the science of work, showing us how to utilize our energy efficiently and purposefully, recognizing that work is inevitable but should be directed towards the highest goal of freedom.

One key principle of Karma Yoga is to work incessantly without attachment, maintaining a sense of detachment from the fruits of our actions. This detachment, known as **Vairâgya** or non-attachment, is the foundation of all Yogas. It is not about renouncing external possessions but about liberating the mind from selfish desires. By performing work selflessly and offering the results to the divine, we break the chains of attachment and achieve true freedom. This principle is beautifully encapsulated in the teaching: "Work incessantly, but give up all attachment to work."

Women of India

The role of women in India is deeply intertwined with the ideals of **Karma Yoga** and societal values. The ideal woman in India is often envisioned as the mother, embodying selflessness, sacrifice, and unconditional love. This reverence for motherhood is reflected in the societal norms and religious practices, where the mother is considered the most revered figure. In Indian homes, the mother holds a position of supreme authority and respect, often seen as the central figure who nurtures and sustains the family.

Indian society, with its diverse castes and customs, has unique traditions regarding women's roles. The caste system, though complex and often

> **Fun Fact:**
>
> **Narendranath Datta's Journey to Becoming Swami Vivekananda:** Born into a well-off Bengali family, Narendranath Datta's life was marked by spiritual awakening and social service. His journey to becoming Swami Vivekananda reflected his deep spiritual quest and mission to awaken humanity.

criticized, has historically dictated social order and relationships. Women in different castes have varied experiences, with customs and expectations shaping their lives significantly. For instance, in higher castes, widows are often not allowed to remarry, which is seen as a form of social sacrifice, while in lower castes, the dynamics might be different.

Education and cultural norms for women have evolved, with increasing emphasis on higher education and empowerment. The ideal of motherhood, however, remains central, influencing how women perceive their roles and responsibilities. The intersection of traditional values and modern aspirations continues to shape the lives of Indian women, balancing between societal expectations and individual freedoms.

Soul, God, and Religion

The essence of **Karma Yoga** and the pursuit of freedom are intrinsically linked to the understanding of the soul, God, and religion. The soul, in its purest form, is free and unattached, bound only by the illusions and attachments of the material world. Religion, as understood in the context of **Karma Yoga**, begins where the material universe ends. True religion involves transcending the transient joys and sorrows of the world, seeking the infinite freedom that lies beyond.

God is perceived as the ultimate reality, the infinite being from which the universe emerges and into which it dissolves. This cyclical process of creation and dissolution is driven by the law of causation, which governs the material world but does not bind the divine essence. The ultimate goal of human existence, according to **Karma Yoga**, is to realize this divine essence within ourselves, transcending the limitations of the body and mind.

By understanding the nature of the soul and its relationship with God, individuals can perform actions selflessly, seeing themselves as instruments of the divine will. This realization transforms work into a form of worship, where every action is an offering to the divine, free from the bonds of attachment and desire. Thus, **Karma Yoga** not only provides a path to personal freedom but also aligns individual actions with the universal purpose, creating a harmonious existence in tune with the divine order.

Swami Vivekananda letter 2nd Nov 1893

5

Foundations of Hinduism

*The Hindu Religion, What Is Religion,
Vedic Religious Ideals, Reason and Religion
(Delivered in England)*

The Hindu Religion

The Hindu religion is vast and complex, encompassing a wide range of beliefs and practices. As one quote poignantly states, *"Truth has always been universal."* This universality is reflected in the Hindu belief that all religions contain elements of truth. The essence of Hinduism is rooted in the ancient Vedas, derived from the word "Vid," meaning "to know." These texts convey the immortality of the soul and the pursuit of a stable equilibrium amidst the ever-changing universe. The Vedanta philosophy teaches that man's soul is independent and immortal, embodying divinity within each individual. *"The soul is God and every human being has a perfect divinity within himself."* This belief encourages the manifestation of one's inner divinity, emphasizing the importance of teaching children that they are inherently divine.

What Is Religion

Religion, as explored in Hinduism, goes beyond mere rituals and traditions. It embodies the quest for freedom and understanding.

"This freedom that distinguishes us from mere machines is what we are all striving for." The goal of all religious effort is to attain perfect freedom, a concept that underlies all forms of worship. From the worship of tribal gods and ancestors to the acknowledgment of an omnipotent, omnipresent deity, the journey is marked by a constant struggle for liberation. The concept of God in Vedanta, known as Sat-chit-ânanda (Existence-Knowledge-Bliss), represents the highest ideal of freedom and knowledge.

Vedic Religious Ideals

The Vedic hymns are some of the oldest expressions of religious thought, praising various gods like Indra, Varuna, and Mitra. Despite their mythological aspects, these deities often embody higher philosophical concepts. For instance, Indra, initially portrayed as a thunderer who battles demons, is later elevated to a being of omnipresence and omnipotence. Similarly, Varuna, the god of the air and waters, is depicted as a divine ruler with omniscient powers. This evolution reflects the Vedic tendency to abstract and elevate the divine to a higher philosophical level, moving from polytheistic worship to a more unified monotheistic idea: *"That which exists is One; sages call It by various names."* This profound realization has fostered an environment in India where diverse religious beliefs coexist peacefully, free from persecution.

Reason and Religion

A discourse between the sages Nârada and Sanatkumâra highlights the primacy of knowledge that leads to the realization of Brahman, the supreme reality. This conversation underscores the notion that true religious knowledge transcends the empirical sciences, encompassing eternal truths. Religion, often seen as supreme knowledge, claims a higher authority due to its eternal nature. However, this has led to conflicts with secular knowledge, which relies on reason and empirical evidence. The question arises: *"Is religion to justify itself by the discoveries of reason through which every other science justifies itself?"* The Vedanta philosophy offers a path that integrates reason with religious belief, proposing that the ultimate generalization and evolution of all things lead back to Brahman, the infinite, impersonal reality that underlies all existence.

In summary, 4 of the Foundations of Hinduism delves into the profound depths of the Hindu religion, exploring its essence, the nature of religion itself, the lofty ideals found in Vedic hymns, and the interplay between reason and faith. Through these discussions, Hinduism presents a framework that encourages the recognition of divinity within oneself, the pursuit of knowledge, and the harmonious coexistence of diverse beliefs.

**Vivekananda in Belur Math
19 June 1899**

6

Religious Philosophy

*The Free Soul (Delivered in New York, 1896),
Unity, The Goal of Religion (Delivered in
New York, 1896), One Existence Appearing
as Many, Christ, The Messenger (Delivered
at Los Angeles, California, 1900)*

The Free Soul (Delivered in New York, 1896)

The concept of the free soul according to the Sânkhya philosophy delves into the duality of existence—Nature and souls. The Sânkhyas assert that there are an infinite number of souls which, being simple, cannot die and must therefore be separate from Nature. Nature itself is seen as constantly changing and manifesting various phenomena, whereas the soul, according to the Sankhyas, is inactive and separate from these changes. Liberation, in this framework, involves the soul realizing that it is not part of Nature. Despite being separate from Nature, the soul is considered omnipresent due to its simple and indivisible nature, which cannot be limited by time, space, or causation.

The Vedantists offer a critical perspective on this duality, suggesting that the analysis of the Sânkhyas is incomplete. They argue that if both Nature and the soul are absolute, it would result in two absolutes, an impossibility. Vedanta posits that the sentient Being, which the Sankhyas recognize as necessary for making the mind think and Nature work, is what they call God. Consequently, this universe is not different from God; it is God who has become the universe. God is seen as both the instrumental and material cause of the universe, indicating that everything that exists is an expression of God.

Stamp of Vivekananda Rock Memorial, Kanyakumari, built in honour of Swami Vivekananda (1863-1902), who attained enlightenment on the rock

Credits: India Post, Government of India, GODL-India <https://data.gov.in/sites/default/files/Gazette_Notification_OGDL.pdf>, via Wikimedia Commons

The second step in Vedanta is the identification of souls as parts of God. Vedanta goes further, stating that each soul is not merely a part but the whole Infinite Brahman. This raises the question of how the infinite can have parts, leading to the conclusion that the apparent multiplicity of souls is an illusion. Just as the sun reflected in millions of globules of water appears as millions of suns, all souls are reflections of the one Infinite Being. The real "I" is the undivided, infinite God, and all individual identities are mere illusions caused by the network of time, space, and causation.

Liberation, according to Vedanta, is realizing that we are not different from God. The soul's bondage is an illusion, akin to clouds passing across the sky, and the realization of the soul's true nature brings about freedom, transforming one into a Jivanmukta, living-free even while in the body. This understanding leads to a life free of fear, realizing the non-existence of worldly illusions. The ultimate knowledge is that the self is the whole of God, not a part, leading to a state where all delusions vanish, and one realizes their eternal, unchanging nature.

Unity, the Goal of Religion (Delivered in New York, 1896)

Religion is not a mere speculative endeavor but an intrinsic aspect of human existence, inherently linked to the very constitution of the human mind. The search for the infinite unknown, which lies beyond the boundaries of the known and the knowable, drives humanity towards religion. This pursuit of the unknown is a fundamental part of human nature, inseparable from life and thought. As long as a man thinks, this struggle for understanding beyond the tangible world must continue, giving rise to various forms of religion.

In the rational and intellectual universe of senses, the quest for knowledge naturally extends into the metaphysical realm, seeking to understand the underlying unity behind all phenomena. Religion, therefore, becomes essential for human progress, fostering spiritual thought that propels intellectual and material advancements. True religion transcends immediate material concerns, aiming to elevate the soul towards eternal bliss and knowledge. It is the quest for this

Swami Vivekananda (1863-1902) in the year 1900 at San Francisco, California, United States.

deeper understanding that distinguishes man from animals, making religion the foundation of human progress.

The ultimate goal of religion, according to Hindu philosophy, is realizing the unity within us. This unity signifies the culmination of all progress, where the soul returns to its divine origin, having found the perfect knowledge that lies within the realization of its oneness with God. The idea that man is infinitely progressing towards an unattainable perfection is seen as absurd. True motion in the universe is circular, not linear, returning to its starting point. Hence, the journey of the soul is a return to God, the source of all existence.

Knowledge, in its highest form, is finding this unity. The diversity of religious forms and practices across the world represents different stages in the journey towards this ultimate truth. Each religion, regardless of its external forms, is a path leading towards the realization of this unity. The Vedanta philosophy, which extends the Sankhya's conclusions, seeks this final unity, viewing the entire universe as an expression of the One Infinite Being.

> **Fun Fact:**
> **Establishing the Ramakrishna Mission:**
> In 1897, Swami Vivekananda founded the Ramakrishna Mission, dedicated to social service and the dissemination of Ramakrishna's teachings.

One Existence Appearing as Many

Renunciation is a central theme across various paths of Yoga. Whether it is the Karmi (worker), the Bhakta (devotee), the Yogi, or the Jnâni (philosopher), each path involves a form of renunciation aimed at realizing the soul's separateness from Nature. The Karmi renounces the fruits of work, the

Bhakta renounces all lesser loves for the love of the divine, the Yogi renounces experiences to understand the soul's eternal separateness from Nature, and the Jnâni renounces everything based on the philosophy that Nature itself never existed in reality.

Happiness, often the measure of utility, finds its highest form in the knowledge of the Self. For the Jnâni, this knowledge represents the highest utility because it brings the greatest happiness. Physical or sensory gratifications are seen as inferior forms of happiness compared to the bliss of self-knowledge. The journey towards this knowledge involves a deep understanding that all existence is one, and the perception of diversity is a result of ignorance and illusion.

Swami Vivekananda 2013 stamp of India

Credits: India Post, Government of India, GODL-India <https://data.gov.in/sites/default/files/Gazette_Notification_OGDL.pdf>, via Wikimedia Commons

The Advaitist philosophy explains the varied religious experiences as hallucinations of the mind. Heaven, hell, rebirth—all are projections of the mind's desires and fears. True existence is the unchanging Atman, omnipresent and eternal. This realization dispels the illusions of birth, death, and worldly change, leading to a state of eternal peace. The world, with its perceived dualities, is an illusion; the only reality is the One Infinite Being.

The practical approach for the Jnâni involves a process of constant assertion and meditation on the truth of the Self. This involves rejecting all thoughts that identify with the body or mind and affirming the truth of being the Infinite Brahman. The realization of this truth leads to the dissolution of all fears and attachments, resulting in the ultimate freedom of the soul.

Christ, the Messenger (Delivered at Los Angeles, California, 1900)

The life and teachings of Christ exemplify the embodiment of divine energy, enduring through ages. Christ's life reflects the culmination of his race's spiritual journey, embodying the highest ideals and propelling future generations towards divine realization. His ministry, though brief, left an indelible impact on the world, unfolding over centuries and continuing to influence humanity profoundly.

> **Fun Fact:**
> **A Prophetic Prediction:** Remarkably, Swami Vivekananda predicted that he would not live past the age of 40. This prediction, made with a sense of calm acceptance, reflected his deep spiritual insight and detachment from the physical realm. His passing at the age of 39 seemed to fulfil this prophecy.

In conclusion, the exploration of these religious philosophies highlights the profound unity underlying all existence. The teachings of Vedanta and Christ converge in their emphasis on the realization of the divine within, transcending the illusions of the material world. This realization is the ultimate goal of all religious and spiritual endeavors, leading to eternal peace and liberation.

7

Indian Religious Thought

Indian Religious Thought, The Methods and Purpose of Religion, The Nature of the Soul and Its Goal

Indian Religious Thought: Methods and Purpose

In studying the religions of the world, we generally find two methods of procedure. One is from God to man, typical of the Semitic group of religions, where the idea of God comes almost from the very first, without any idea of the soul. The other is through man to God, which is peculiarly Aryan. The Aryans first began with the soul, and as their idea of the soul became clearer, so did their idea of God. The Vedas always inquired through the soul, seeking divinity inside one's own self.

The Nature of the Soul and Its Goal

The earliest idea is that a man, when he dies, is not annihilated. Something lives and continues after death. Comparing the Egyptians, Babylonians, and ancient Hindus, we find the idea of a double or spiritual body. The Aryans believed in the soul as a separate entity from the body, leading to the custom of burning the dead. The soul is seen as pure, perfect, omnipotent, and omniscient, manifesting itself externally according to the mind's clarity. The goal of the soul among all Indian sects is liberation—freedom from limitations, internal or external, achieving infinite nature.

Photo of Swami Vivekananda in Jaipur (between 1885–1895)
Credits: Ramakrishna Mission Delhi, Public domain, via Wikimedia Commons

8

Insights from the Gita

Thoughts on the Gita, The Story of Jada Bharata (Delivered in California), On Fanaticism, Work is Worship, Work Without Motive

Thoughts on the Gita

The Gita, part of the Mahabharata, requires several key considerations to understand properly. Questions arise about its authorship, attributed to Veda-Vyasa, and whether it was an interpolation. Additionally, the historical existence of Krishna, the great war of Kurukshetra, and the reality of Arjuna and others are points of inquiry.

1. **Authorship and Antiquity**:
   - The title "Vyasa" was common, and discerning the true author, whether Badarayana Vyasa or Dvaipayana Vyasa, is complex. The Gita gained prominence primarily due to Shankaracharya's commentary. Earlier commentaries, like that of Bodhayana, are shrouded in uncertainty.
2. **Historical Krishna**:
   - The personality of Krishna is debated. Ancient texts like the Chandogya Upanishad mention Krishna, son of Devaki, while the Mahabharata portrays him as the king of Dwarka. The Vishnu Purana and Bhagavata describe

his playful interactions with the Gopis, casting doubt on these narratives' historical accuracy.
3. **Kurukshetra War**:
   - There is no conclusive evidence for the war, though it's clear a significant conflict between the Kurus and Panchalas occurred. Some view the Kurukshetra War allegorically, representing the inner struggle between good and evil within man.
4. **Existence of Arjuna and Others**:
   - Doubts about the historicity of Arjuna and others arise from ancient texts like the Shatapatha Brahmana, which mentions Ashvamedha Yajna performers without naming Arjuna or his brothers.

Ultimately, these historical inquiries, while intriguing, do not detract from the Gita's spiritual teachings. The Gita's core message harmonizes Yoga, Jnana, and Bhakti, advocating for work without desire or attachment, embodying the spirit of Nishkama Karma.

The Story of Jada Bharata (Delivered in California)

King Bharata, after renouncing his throne, retreated to the forest to meditate on the Self. He saved a fawn from a river, nurturing it back to health. This attachment to the deer distracted him from his meditation. Upon his death, his thoughts were fixed on the deer, leading to his rebirth as a deer. Even as a deer, he retained memories of his past life, eventually being reborn as a Brahmin's son.

Living as a Jatismara (one who remembers past lives), he avoided worldly entanglements, behaving as if inert or insane to escape life's snares. His profound wisdom revealed itself when he was conscripted to carry a king's palanquin. Addressing the king, he expounded on the nature of the self, leading the king to recognize his true sage identity.

Jada Bharata's story illustrates the importance of detachment and constant remembrance of the Self, transcending the cycle of birth and death through unwavering devotion and wisdom.

On Fanaticism

Fanaticism, whether over trivial matters like smoking or significant issues like social reforms, often stems from selfishness and lack of understanding. Fanatics fail to see the broader picture, focusing narrowly on their beliefs while disregarding others' perspectives.

Swami Vivekananda criticizes this narrow-mindedness, advocating for a balanced approach to life. True reform and compassion arise not from fanatic zeal but from genuine understanding and sympathy for others' struggles.

Work is Worship

The highest form of work is done without attachment, recognizing that all actions are a form of worship. This profound concept signifies that every task we undertake, no matter how mundane or grand, is a sacred offering to the divine. The world, in its vast and intricate design, operates under the divine will. Hence, it does not require our assistance in the literal sense; instead, we are granted the honor of participating in its divine symphony. By perceiving work as worship, we transcend the ego's desires and align our actions with a higher purpose.

When we view work as worship, our motives shift from self-centered goals to a broader, more altruistic vision. This perspective eradicates selfish motives and fosters a spirit of humility and devotion. We no longer work merely for personal gain or recognition but for the upliftment of others and the fulfillment of our spiritual duties. This transformation in attitude not only enhances our inner peace but also contributes positively to society.

In this divine engagement, every action becomes a pathway to spiritual growth. Whether we are performing our professional duties, helping a neighbor, or simply tending to our daily chores, each act is infused with a sense of sacredness and purpose. This holistic approach to work fosters an environment where love, compassion, and dedication thrive, creating a ripple effect that touches every aspect of our lives and those around us.

Moreover, the recognition that we are instruments in the divine plan instills a sense of responsibility and reverence for all forms of life. It encourages us to approach our duties with meticulous care and integrity, knowing that our work, no matter how small, contributes to the greater good. This realization leads to a more fulfilling and content life, where our efforts are harmonized with the universe's divine rhythm.

Work Without Motive

Swami Vivekananda's address on "Work without Motive" delves deep into the essence of Karma-Yoga, as taught in the Gita. This doctrine emphasizes performing actions without any attachment to the fruits of those actions. True work, according to this teaching, is performed with a pure heart and selfless intent, focusing solely on the welfare of others. By doing so, we engage in activities that are free from the shackles of personal gain and desire, which ultimately leads to spiritual liberation.

January 30, 1887, in Baranagar Math, Kolkata, India.
Swami Vivekananda with Ramakrishna devotees.

The essence of working without motive lies in the principle of Nishkama Karma, which advocates for action performed without any expectation of rewards. This selfless action is the hallmark of true spiritual practice, where the doer is detached from the results, good or bad. By embracing this approach, one attains a state of inner tranquility and freedom, as the mind is no longer disturbed by success or failure.

Swami Vivekananda elucidates that working without motive does not imply a lack of passion or commitment. On the contrary, it requires intense focus and dedication, where the individual's ego is dissolved in the act of service. This form of work is driven by a higher consciousness, where the individual sees themselves as a mere instrument of the divine will. The focus is on the action itself, rather than its outcome, which liberates the soul from the bondage of karma.

9

Preparations for Higher Life

Sadhanas or Preparations for Higher Life,
The Cosmos and the Self, Who is a Real Guru?
On Art, On Language

Sadhanas Or Preparations For Higher Life

Embarking on the journey towards higher life, or spiritual advancement, demands rigorous and disciplined preparation, commonly referred to as Sadhanas. The initial and most critical focus should be on achieving mastery and control over one's own body. A common pitfall is becoming overly preoccupied with correcting others, while true spiritual progress starts within us.

Self-Discipline and Bodily Control

Historically, there was a time when humans had greater control over bodily functions such as the liver and heart, and even the ability to shake the skin like certain animals. This control can be reclaimed through sheer hard practice, highlighting the importance of physical discipline. By consciously bringing submerged activities back under control, one can lay a solid foundation for spiritual growth.

Social and Spiritual Balance

While this bodily control is essential for social well-being, it is equally important to focus on spiritual liberation. This aspect of study aims to free the soul, enabling it to transcend the mundane and march onwards to the superconscious state. Achieving this state transforms an individual into a divine being, capable of uncovering the universe's deepest secrets. The ultimate goal is to pass beyond the dualities of life and death, recognizing and becoming one with the Real.

The Importance of Quietude

A peaceful and quiet life is crucial for spiritual development. Engaging in constant worldly activities and struggles makes it difficult to attain higher states of consciousness. However, with earnest desire and effort, even challenging circumstances can change within a single lifetime. Our deepest desires shape our reality, and this is evident in the way our bodies develop senses like eyes and ears in response to external stimuli. A serene environment, free from the distractions and anxieties of daily life, provides the ideal setting for meditation and spiritual growth.

Meditation: The Path to Spiritual Life

Meditation is the cornerstone of the journey towards higher life. It allows the mind to transcend material existence and touch the soul. Regular meditation fosters a sense of non-attachment and helps us realize that the body, while necessary, can also be an obstacle in spiritual practice. By consistently affirming "I am the Spirit," we train ourselves to become witnesses rather than participants in the external world's trials and tribulations.

The Power of Non-Attachment

Developing non-attachment is essential. It is like appreciating a painting of a terrible scene without being affected by it, recognizing it as an artistic representation rather than reality. Similarly, in life, we must learn to witness events without becoming emotionally entangled. This perspective allows us to maintain peace and spiritual focus amidst the world's chaos.

Struggle and Determination

The struggle for spiritual excellence must be as intense, if not more, than the struggle for material success. This path is not for the faint-hearted but for those who can endure hardships and keep moving forward despite obstacles. The soul grows stronger through challenges, emerging triumphant and self-realized.

The Value of Struggle

Struggle and determination are indispensable in spiritual practice. It is through facing and overcoming challenges that the soul becomes robust and resilient. Just as people expend enormous energy in the pursuit of wealth, which is fleeting, we should invest even more energy in attaining spiritual freedom, which is eternal.

A commemorative postage stamp on Swami Vivekananda was issued on 17 Jan 1963 by India Post.

Credits: India Post, Government of India, GODL-India <https://data.gov.in/sites/default/files/Gazette_Notification_OGDL.pdf>, via Wikimedia Commons

The Cosmos And The Self

The relationship between the cosmos and the self is profound and intrinsic. The universe and all within it, including the self, undergo cycles of evolution and involution. Each form in nature, from the tiniest seed to the vast cosmos, goes through a process of becoming more gross before eventually returning to a finer state.

Cycles of Evolution and Involution

Our earth, for example, emerged from a nebulous state, crystallized into its current form, and will eventually disintegrate back into a nebulous form. This cyclical process has been ongoing since time immemorial. Every evolution is preceded by an involution, where the entire form exists in a subtle state before manifesting in a grosser form.

Universal Intelligence

The culmination of the universe's evolution is intelligence, which also marks its beginning. This universal intelligence, often referred to as God, manifests through us and everything around us. Understanding this connection helps us grasp our true nature and the essence of existence beyond physical and mental boundaries.

Who Is A Real Guru?

A real Guru is a beacon of spiritual force, born to guide others towards enlightenment. This spiritual energy is transmitted through generations of disciples. True spiritual guidance requires complete humility and surrender to the Guru, shedding any sense of personal spiritual wisdom. The Guru's role is crucial as they lead us towards spiritual perfection, which we cannot achieve on our own due to our limited understanding.

The Guru-Disciple Relationship

The relationship between a Guru and disciple is sacred. A disciple must surrender completely to the Guru's guidance, recognizing their own limitations and the Guru's superior spiritual insight. This humility and self-surrender are vital for spiritual illumination and growth.

On Art

Art, in its truest form, is a representation of the ideal rather than a mere imitation of nature. Greek art, with its focus on minute realism, contrasts with Indian art, which strives to depict the transcendental. True art remains grounded in nature but rises above it to express higher ideals.

The Purpose of Art

Art is about conveying beauty and ideas, distinguishing it from mere structural creation. It should elevate the mind and spirit, transcending the physical to touch upon the ideal and the sublime. Art that loses touch with nature degenerates, but art that remains grounded while aspiring higher achieves true greatness.

On Language

Simplicity and expressiveness are key to effective language. The ideal language should convey thoughts clearly and colloquially, much like the teachings of great spiritual masters. Efforts to refine language should focus on maintaining its natural flow and expressive power, avoiding overly complex and artificial constructs.

Language as a Tool for Communication

Language must serve its primary purpose: to communicate ideas effectively. Overcomplicating language can hinder understanding and dilute the message. Therefore, the best language is one that is simple, direct, and capable of expressing profound thoughts clearly.

Swami Vivekananda in Shillong, India in 1901, this is one of the last known photographs of Swami Vivekananda (1863-1902).

By integrating these preparations and understandings into our lives, we pave the way for higher spiritual achievements, aligning our daily actions with the pursuit of eternal truths and self-realization. Through self-discipline, quietude, meditation, and the guidance of a real Guru, we can navigate the complexities of the cosmos and our own selves, striving towards the ultimate goal of spiritual liberation and unity with the divine.

10

The Life of a Sannyasin

The Sannyasin, On Bhakti-Yoga, Ishvara and Brahman, On Jnana-Yoga

The Sannyasin

A Sannyasin, as explained by Swami Vivekananda, is someone who has fulfilled the duties and obligations of their life stage and seeks a spiritual existence, abandoning worldly pursuits such as possession, fame, or power. With an understanding of the world's impermanence, strife, and misery, a Sannyasin turns away from these illusions to seek the true, the eternal love, and refuge. This renunciation (Sannyasa) involves giving up all worldly positions, property, and names, and embarking on a life of self-sacrifice, continually seeking spiritual knowledge. Through years of meditation, discipline, and inquiry, a Sannyasin gains wisdom and insight, eventually becoming a teacher to others.

Swami Vivekananda Memorial Plaque

Credits: Simon Harriyott, CC BY 2.0 <https:// creativecommons.org/licenses/ by/2.0>, via Wikimedia Commons

A Sannyasin does not belong to any single religion; their life is characterized by independent thought that draws from all religions. They live a life of realization, not merely theory or belief, much less dogma.

On Bhakti-Yoga

The dualist perspective holds that morality is dependent on the fear of divine punishment, likening humans to cab-horses that move only with the whip. However, Vivekananda argues that true religion is about realizing the idea of God, beyond just the spelling of words or doctrines. The personal God, an objectification of the Self, emerges through the haze of Maya and is the highest form of that shadow, helping to break the chains of worldly imaginations.

Bhakti, or devotion, is not about bargaining with God for daily needs but is a higher state of religious practice, transcending even the desire for heaven. The essence of Bhakti is to realize the divine presence within, not to indulge in sensory pleasures or material comforts.

Ishvara and Brahman

In Vedantic philosophy, Ishvara represents the collective total of all individual souls, akin to how the human body is a unit composed of individual cells. Ishvara is dependent on the existence of individual souls (Jivas) and vice versa, making them coexistent. Ishvara embodies omnipotence and omniscience as a totality, while Brahman transcends these attributes, being the singular principle running through all existence. Brahman is beyond composition and differentiation, and every individual realization of Brahman affirms its singular, all-encompassing nature.

On Jnana-Yoga

Religion, in essence, is learning to play consciously in life, guided by the same universal laws that govern the cosmos. The idea of immortality is inherent in humans, and life, coupled with death, forms an inseparable continuum. Progress is not linear but circular, with every soul projected from a common divine center, destined to return after completing its journey.

Each soul, though omnipresent, is conscious at a single point, which manifests as the body. Death merely signifies a change in this conscious center, and realization of God means transcending the limited body-centered consciousness.

The pursuit of Jnana (knowledge) involves understanding that the diversity we perceive is an illusion created by the mind. The real unity lies beyond this differentiation, and the goal is to perceive this underlying oneness. The true test of renunciation is to live in the world without being of it, maintaining inner detachment while engaging with life's duties.

Swami Vivekananda (London 1896).

11

Philosophical Teachings

The Cause of Illusion, Evolution, Buddhism and Vedanta, On the Vedanta Philosophy, Law and Freedom

The Cause of Illusion

The enigma of Mâyâ, or illusion, has puzzled thinkers for millennia. The central question is: what causes Mâyâ? The response is that this question itself is paradoxical and thus unanswerable in the conventional sense. The Absolute, by definition, cannot be acted upon or influenced by anything else. It is uncaused, implying that nothing external can affect it. Therefore, asking what caused the Absolute to manifest as the conditioned is contradictory.

Our position holds that the Absolute appears as the relative only in the context of Mâyâ. The Unconditioned becomes conditioned in the framework of time, space, and causation, which are constructs of Mâyâ. Ignorance, or Avidya, is what creates the illusion. The question of what

Fun Fact:

Mastery of Multiple Languages: Swami Vivekananda was fluent in multiple languages, including Bengali, English, and Sanskrit. His linguistic skills allowed him to communicate with diverse audiences and access a vast array of spiritual and philosophical texts.

causes the Absolute to change into the relative is invalid because it attempts to apply conditioned logic to the Unconditioned.

In the realm of the Absolute, there is no time, space, or causation, thus no scope for change or influence. The illusion arises from our ignorance, not from any causal interaction. The Absolute is beyond the domain of knowledge. Asserting the Absolute's nature involves transcending the plane of ordinary knowing. The knower cannot be objectified; the self cannot perceive itself as an object. This concept is essential in understanding the philosophical teachings about immortality and the nature of the self.

Swami Vivekananda's Ancestral House, Cultural Centre and museum in north Kolkata, India.

Credits: Biswarup Ganguly, CC BY-SA 4.0 <https://creativecommons.org/licenses/by-sa/4.0>, via Wikimedia Commons

Evolution

Indian thought, particularly that of the Yogis, offers a perspective on evolution that closely parallels modern scientific views, yet with unique insights. Evolution, according to Yogic philosophy, involves the unfolding of inherent divine qualities, unimpeded by external struggles. Patanjali's idea of "infilling of nature" suggests that the divinity within us naturally manifests as obstacles are removed.

A stamp from Swami Vivekananda (1863-1902) to the Centenary of Chicago Address before the World Parliament of Religions, released 1993 in India.

Credits: India Post, Government of India, GODL-India <https://data.gov.in/sites/default/files/Gazette_Notification_OGDL.pdf>, via Wikimedia Commons

This view negates the necessity of competition and struggle for progress, contrary to the modern concept of survival of the fittest. Instead, it posits that evolution is an internal process driven by the inherent momentum of the soul. The struggles and evils we perceive are seen as unnecessary hindrances that can be eliminated, allowing for a calm, natural progression towards divinity.

The theory of Patanjali presents a hopeful outlook, rejecting the notion that competition is essential for evolution. Historical analysis reveals that wars and conflicts have often impeded human progress. According to Patanjali, the natural evolution of the soul towards divinity is an inevitable process, unaffected by external conflicts and struggles. This inner momentum is likened to a river flowing towards the sea, unhindered by external obstacles.

Buddhism and Vedanta

The Vedanta philosophy serves as the bedrock of Buddhism and other Indian philosophies, albeit with some distinctions. While traditional Hindus may view Buddhists as heretics, there is an underlying attempt within Vedanta to harmonize all beliefs, including Buddhism. Vedanta does not see a dichotomy between the noumenal (ultimate reality) and the phenomenal (perceived reality); rather, it views them as one. The phenomenal world is a misperception of the noumenal.

Buddhism's focus on phenomena and the role of desire in creating reality contrasts with Vedanta, which sees will and desire as secondary phenomena. Vedanta posits that the ultimate reality is beyond will, which is itself a compound, dependent on external stimuli and thus not absolute. The will, according to Vedanta, is a manifestation of a deeper reality. This fundamental disagreement with the will-theory of German philosophers like Schopenhauer underscores Vedanta's unique perspective on the nature of reality.

> **Fun Fact:**
> **Inspiration for the Indian Freedom Movement:** Swami Vivekananda inspired Indian freedom leaders, promoting self-reliance and empowerment.

On the Vedanta Philosophy

Vedanta philosophy asserts that the soul is neither born nor dies and that reincarnation is a misinterpretation of changes in nature, not the soul itself. Each soul is omnipresent and eternal, unchanging amidst the apparent cycles of birth and death. This philosophy holds that true freedom and realization come from understanding the soul's divine nature, which is beyond good and evil.

Vedanta emphasizes the necessity of moral and ethical conduct as means to attain spiritual freedom. The ultimate goal is the realization of one's divinity, transcending all dualities and attaining a state of eternal bliss and knowledge. This realization is described as Nirvana, which can be attained here and now, without waiting for death.

The Vedanta philosophy promotes the idea that we are all inherently divine and that our true nature is beyond good and evil. This understanding leads to a state of inner peace and bliss, where the individual soul merges with the universal soul, realizing its oneness with all existence.

Monument to Swami Vivekananda in Mumbai, India

Credits: A. Savin, FAL, via Wikimedia Commons

The path to this realization involves recognizing the divinity within all beings and actions, leading to a state where one is unaffected by external circumstances and embodies the divine in everyday life. This realization of freedom is described as the ultimate goal of human life, where the individual soul attains its true nature and experiences eternal bliss and freedom.

The tableau of West Bengal on the theme 'Obeisance to Swami Vivekanand' passes through the Rajpath during the full-dress rehearsal for the Republic Day Parade 2013, in New Delhi on January 23, 2013.

Credits: Ministry of Defence (GODL-India), GODL-India <https://data.gov.in/sites/default/files/Gazette_Notification_OGDL.pdf>, via Wikimedia Commons

12

From Colombo to Almora

The Religion We Are Born In, Sannyasa:
Its Ideal and Practice, The Sages of India,
The Future of India,

The Religion We Are Born In

At an open-air meeting convened at Dacca on the 31st March 1901, Swamiji delivered an impassioned speech on the religion we inherit at birth. This lecture, translated from a Bengali report of a disciple, highlighted the profound spiritual advancements made by ancient India and cautioned against complacency rooted in past glories. Swamiji emphasized that while it is essential to recall our ancient greatness, it should not lead to stagnation but should inspire us to strive for even greater spiritual heights.

Swamiji discussed the common grounds of agreement within Hinduism despite its apparent diversity. He pointed out that different sects—Advaitists, Vishishtadvaitists, and Dvaitists—hold varying beliefs, from the concept of God incarnations to image worship and the doctrine of the formless. Despite these differences, unity can be found in the rejection of beef consumption among Hindus and in the shared reverence for the Vedas.

Vivekananda Rock Memorial, Kanyakumari, last south land of India. It was built in honour of Swami Vivekananda (1863-1902), who is said to have attained enlightenment on the rock.
Credits: Milan S Thottathil, CC BY-SA 4.0 <https://creativecommons.org/licenses/by-sa/4.0>, via Wikimedia Commons

The Vedas, divided into Karma Kanda and Jnana Kanda, form the basis of Hinduism. While the Karma Kanda has largely fallen into disuse, the Jnana Kanda, comprising the Upanishads or Vedanta, remains the cornerstone of Hindu thought. Swamiji asserted that all Hindu sects, regardless of their specific beliefs, must base their doctrines on the authority of the Vedanta. He underscored the belief that the Vedas are not merely ancient texts but are seen as an infinite mine of divine wisdom, discovered by the Rishis.

Swamiji elaborated on the significance of Rishis, who, regardless of their birth or background, attained realization of Dharma through proper means. He highlighted the egalitarian nature of spiritual attainment, encouraging even the present-day Kulin Brahmins to strive for Rishihood. The Veda, he declared, is the ultimate authority, accessible to all, and should be revered and studied in every household.

Sannyasa: Its Ideal and Practice

On the eve of his second voyage to the West, Swamiji addressed the junior Sannyasins of the Belur Math. In this parting address, he delineated the ideal of Sannyasa, characterizing it as "the love of death" in a metaphorical sense—embracing self-sacrifice for the greater good. He stressed that Sannyasins should strive to benefit others, turning every action, whether eating or reading, into an act of sacrifice for the well-being of humanity.

Swami Vivekananda temple at Belur Math,
at the place where he was cremated.

Swamiji called for a balance between idealism and practicality, warning against the extremes of too lofty ideals that weaken a nation and excessive practicality that reduces one to brute existence. He urged the Sannyasins to combine intense meditation with practical activities, such as cultivating fields or selling produce, embodying both intellectual and physical labor. He emphasized that the ultimate goal of the institution is to create strong, compassionate individuals who embody both strength and tenderness.

> **Fun Fact:**
> **The Practical Application of Vedanta:** Swami Vivekananda emphasized living Vedanta's principles in daily life, encouraging virtue, compassion, and service.

He highlighted the importance of obedience and discipline within the Sangha, encouraging members to crush disobedience and foster a deep regard for the community. Swamiji's vision was of individuals who are both free in spirit and obedient to their duties, ready to serve the world with unwavering commitment and selflessness.

The Sages of India

Swamiji's reflections on the sages of India took the audience back to periods beyond recorded history. He underscored that the Hindu nation has been dedicated to producing sages for thousands of years. Swamiji distinguished between two sets of truths in the scriptures: the eternal truths embodied in the Vedas (Shrutis) and the contextual truths in the Smritis and Puranas. While the Shrutis provide the framework for spiritual life, the Smritis and Puranas offer detailed guidance for specific times and circumstances.

He emphasized that Hinduism's strength lies in its foundation on impersonal principles rather than personal authorities. Swamiji elaborated on the concept of the Rishi,

> **Fun Fact:**
> **Global Recognition through the World Religions Congress:** Swami Vivekananda gained global recognition at the World Religions Congress in Chicago, advocating for religious tolerance and brotherhood.

the seer of thought, whose realization of spiritual truths transcends the sensory world. He encouraged individuals to strive for Rishihood, achieving direct perception of spiritual realities through deep practice and self-realization. Swamiji stressed that true religious life begins only when one attains superconsciousness, moving beyond mere intellectual or ritualistic practices.

The Future of India

Swamiji envisioned a resurgent India, drawing strength from its spiritual heritage. He emphasized the need for unity in religion as the foundation of national identity, arguing that religious ideals form the core of Indian life. Swamiji believed that India's future lay in revitalizing its spiritual traditions and making them accessible to all.

> **Fun Fact:**
> **An Early Departure:** Swami Vivekananda's life was relatively short, as he passed away on July 4, 1902, at the age of 39. Despite his brief lifespan, his impact on the spiritual and social fabric of the world was profound and lasting.

He called for the dissemination of Sanskrit knowledge and spiritual teachings in the vernacular, making them available to the masses. Swamiji stressed the importance of cultural education alongside spiritual teachings, asserting that knowledge alone is insufficient without the depth of culture. He warned against creating new caste divisions and emphasized

Birthplace of Swami Vivekananda–First Floor–Kolkata

Credits: Biswarup Ganguly, CC BY-SA 4.0 <https://creativecommons.org/licenses/by-sa/4.0>, via Wikimedia Commons

the need for widespread education to empower all sections of society.

Swamiji addressed the complex problems facing India, including racial, linguistic, and social differences. He argued that spiritual unity could transcend these divides, fostering a sense of

> **Fun Fact:**
> **Memorial at Belur Math:** Swami Vivekananda was cremated at Belur Math, now a pilgrimage site honouring his life and contributions.

common identity. He urged the audience to draw strength from India's glorious past and use it as a foundation to build a greater future.

He emphasized that India's vitality lies in its spirituality, which must be preserved and strengthened. Swamiji called for the collective effort to rejuvenate the nation, using spiritual teachings to cleanse and invigorate the national life. He believed that a spiritually strong India could withstand and overcome any external challenges.

Vivekananda College for Women, established in 1961, Barisha, Kolkata, West Bengal.

Credits: Salil Kumar Mukherjee, CC BY-SA 4.0 <https://creativecommons.org/licenses/by-sa/4.0>, via Wikimedia Commons